# The Educator

*Countless Ideas
to Teach Students
How to Think*

Teaching Skills of
Bernard F. Nanni

*by Pamela Green-Nanni*

A LeasCon Book

Copyright © 2015 by Pamela M. Green

Published in the United States by Image Ink Publications.

Copy edited by Pamela Green-Nanni
Associate Editor Toni Rodgers

Library of Congress Number:   2016912342
ISBN:   978-1-929219-10-0

First printing:   November 15, 2016
Second printing:  February 20, 2017

Interior artwork: dreamstime.com: Rope Bridge
(Albund), Amazon Rain Forest (Dirk Ercken), Ape
(Isselee, modified), Crocodile (Tratong), Village Houses
(Michael Zysman),  S.A.V.E. (Mark Bonett); Free
Photos Amazon: Hostile Native Tribe; Jamal Muhsin of
Karachi, Pakistan:  handwriting; classroomclipart.com:
blackboard eraser;  Free Hand Puppets Photos Images;
Free Students Wrestling Pictures Images

This book is authored by Pamela Green-Nanni, and
may be obtained through major bookstores or website
http://www.ellenblend.com.

# The Educator

## Table of Contents

# Bernard F. Nanni
## Educational Background

St. David Elementary School
Detroit, Michigan

De La Salle Collegiate High School
Detroit, Michigan

University of Detroit
Bachelor of Science in Education
Detroit, Michigan

Saginaw Valley State College
Master of Arts in Teaching
Saginaw, Michigan

# Preface

This book was written expressly for colleagues and former students of Bernard F. Nanni, family members, and especially for use as a teaching guide and thought starter for educators throughout the nation.

Although Mr. Nanni didn't feel the title of this book was exactly correct because of the uncharacteristic ways in which he taught, my personal assessment is that he taught his students many things about life as he taught the subject matter at hand.

Mr. Nanni looked far beyond teaching as a profession. He took a personal interest in the development of his students, emphasizing the need and their ability to think. Although his methods were not always conventional, he made a lasting impression on students, with many thanking him for their learning experience.

In the most practical way, he stimulated the thinking of his students and presented real-life situations for them to ponder. It cannot be denied that he taught his students "how to think," which he claims is the best thing he could ever teach them.

# Schools and Curriculum

Hutchinson Elementary, Detroit, Michigan, 2nd Grade, Social Studies

Christopher Columbus Elementary, Detroit, Michigan, Physical Education

Ellis Elementary, Center Line, Michigan, 6th Grade, Basketball

Center Line Public Schools, Center Line, Michigan, 6th, 7th and 8th Grades, Softball, and Junior Varsity

East Detroit Public Schools, Eastpointe, Michigan, 6th, 7th and 8th Grades

De La Salle Collegiate High School, Detroit, Michigan, Assistant Coach, Junior Varsity

Catholic Youth Organization, Detroit, Michigan, Football

St. Alphonsus, Dearborn, Michigan, Football

Wolfe Middle School, Center Line, Michigan, Football, Wrestling

Busch Middle School, Center Line, Michigan, Football, Wrestling

# Introduction

Bernard F. Nanni is the proud father of six children and many grandchildren. He always enjoys when they and his wife's children, and all of the grandkids, get together.

As for his career, he was truly an educator. Years after his retirement, he still has dreams of teaching school. He taught $5^{th}$, $6^{th}$ and $7^{th}$ grades for more than 30 years in a public environment, and later, 1 year at a Catholic school. He was also a football coach for fifteen years and taught wrestling for twenty years to $7^{th}$ and $8^{th}$ grade students.

He is so loving of his former career that he still attracts and charms students wherever he goes. He mostly encounters young people working as waitresses that come to his table. He asks

1

them, "Are you going to school?" and "What is your academic field?" He then proceeds to ask them trick questions giving them a lesson in listening.

Here are some of his routine questions:

Nanni: What is your name?

Waitress: Jennifer

Nanni: How do you spell that?

Waitress: J-e-n-n-i-f-e-r.

Nanni: No, that.

He waits for the right answer and the student to smile.

Waitress: Oh, t-h-a-t!

Here's another one.

Nanni: What is the common soft drink that begins with the letter "C"?

Waitress:  Coke

Nanni:  What does a comedian tell?

Waitress:  Joke

Nanni:  What is this called?  (Poking the person next to him.)

Waitress:  Poke

Nanni:  And the white of an egg?

Waitress:  Yolk

Well, the "yolk" is on them, as they quickly answer without thinking.  The white part of an egg is called albumen.

Only one student has answered that question correctly so far, but he continues to ask other questions such as this.

Nanni: Are you good at geography?

Waitress: Somewhat.

Nanni: Okay, there were some travelers in a plane that crashed right at the top of the Appalachian Mountains between Kentucky and Tennessee. Where did they bury the survivors?

Answers varied, but seldom did he get, "You don't bury survivors."

Whenever he could make a joke or make someone laugh, he was happy. One of his sisters said that all he needed was an audience, even an audience of one.

He told me that his father's side of the family was all about fun and laughter, and from what I have seen, this is true. They always have stories to recall, and still enjoy the humor in them.

Of all the waitresses Mr. Nanni queried, only one came back with a riddle for him:

### As I was Going to St. Ives

As I was going to St. Ives,
I met a man with seven wives,
Each wife had seven sacks,
Each sack had seven cats,
Each cat had seven kits:
Kits, cats, sacks, and wives,
How many were there going
To St. Ives?

The answer to the riddle:

Only one man was going to St. Ives!

This is an English nursery rhyme in the form of a riddle, with an origination that goes as far back as 1730. It represents an algorithm for multiplying numbers.

He met the following who were not going:

A man (1) with (7) wives
7 x 7 (49) sacks
7 x 7 x 7 (343) cats
7 x 7 x 7 x 7 (2,401) kits

A total of 2,801 wives, sacks, cats, and kits!

One of Mr. Nanni's daughters, Angela, also became a teacher. She enjoys having him visit some of her classes and to participate in the teaching.

She knows that her father always interjects some form of amusement when he teaches, but together they are able to build on one another's teaching skills.

One of her teacher friends remarked on how proud he was of her and, when he came to visit, how genuinely happy he was to be around the students. She told her that her father was such a delight and obviously gave of himself.

He had a way of taming a classroom full of students. One day he told them to be very quiet, as he had to go to the office for something.

"I want you to prove to me that you are the best class. You can work on your homework, or write poetry, but there should be no talking."

While in the office, the PA system was opened up to his classroom. There was complete silence.

The office administrator listened along with him and said, "There's nobody in there!"

Even Mr. Nanni admitted that some of the students' parents asked for him to be their children's teacher.

Sometimes Angela enlists her father's assistance in setting up a new classroom at the beginning of the term. He loves being a part of her teaching life, and often comments on what an excellent teacher she is. His comment is always, "She far surpasses me in how I taught."

His youngest daughter, Taylor, would also like to teach. She has been gifted with a beautiful voice and the talent to present herself well. She sang *Over the Rainbow* at a family reunion held in Pennsylvania a few years ago, and it was sung so beautifully that I couldn't stop the tears falling from my eyes.

I have told her that she has the voice of angels, as I can hear harmony in just one of her tones. I was so proud of her, as I'm sure all others were in her family.

As Mr. Nanni recalls some of his teaching experiences, he says, "I told my kids, the greatest thing I can ever teach you is how to think."

And that he did. His methods were not always conventional, but most were memorable to his students.

As his wife, I have often been with him when he has encountered a former student who remembers him well, and quite often a particular lesson that was learned.

He and the student reminisce about the funny things that

happened in class, and how the experiences enhanced both of their lives.

One day I went to my credit union to cash a check written to me by Bernard Nanni. The teller, Jennifer Plummer, recognized his name.

She told me how much she enjoyed him as her teacher. In fact, she said, "Having him as a teacher was one of my most memorable experiences. He was a great teacher, and a strong and positive influence on my education."

I later learned that Jennifer was actually a manager of the credit union, and moved on to excel at another firm after I met her.

Her sister, Liz Holzman, also had some kind remarks about his teaching. "He was a great teacher, and was always patient and kind. I was very sensitive, and I felt that he respected that. He helped me get through that awkward teenage stage."

She also stated that religion in schools was starting to get controversial, and I thought he was somewhat of a rebel by always talking about "the big man upstairs."

Another student commented that he tried to gain knowledge from individuals whom he admired, and Mr. Nanni was one of those people.

There were two important things that he learned from him, and one was to never give up on yourself, and to have heart in whatever you do.

He said that Mr. Nanni made a big difference in his life as a student, an athlete, and most importantly as a person. He attributes a lot of his successes to the positive values that Mr. Nanni instilled in him.

While Mr. Nanni was very serious about his teaching, he always managed to bring fun into the classroom. Lesson plans were always there, but loosely followed. He made the students learn because of the creative and stimulating ideas he brought forth.

His love of children, and the desire to see them learn, kept his imagination reeling. "Ideas just came to me," he said, when I asked him about his methods.

One of his students, Anthony Cascianelli, who seemed to struggle academically, was recognized as actually having the aptitude to do better. He always told him that he was his "diamond in the rough," and encouraged him to apply himself.

In the end, Anthony started getting A's and continued to do so from 6<sup>th</sup> grade on through all of junior high school. He ended up stating that he now knows what Mr. Nanni meant. "If you don't believe in yourself, who else will? Always do your best."

Mr. Nanni was happy even when students were able to bring their "D" work up to a "C." If they showed improvement, he knew that he was making a difference.

While not every day was filled with entertainment, he had a way of keeping his students interested and alert. He taught "thinking" as well as the subject matter at hand.

# Game Instructions
# for Learning

## Blackboard Races

The classroom was divided into teams by rows, usually 5 to 6 people per row. Long division problems were written on pieces of paper, and handed out to each row. Each team had a different problem, and the first person in each row had to write the problem on the board. For example:

4,222,000 divided by 65

The second person would do the first step of the division, the third person, the next, and so on. When a mistake was made, the next person up was to say nothing, but correct the error as their step in completing the problem.

The race would be on to complete the division problem first, without error. Students were taught to work together, and to teach one another.

When the first team was done, other team members could challenge the winning row to prove that their answer was correct.

The next person up of the winning team would work the proof on the board by multiplying the divisor and the answer, or quotient, to get the dividend and perhaps a remainder. Terms of the problem were also taught.

| | | |
|---|---|---|
| quotient | | 6 |
| divisor | 3 | 19 |
| dividend | | 18 |
| remainder | | 1 |

If two teams completed the problem at the same time, they would be required to prove each other's answer on the board.

At one time, Mr. Nanni was on a math committee at the school where he was teaching. He was asked to speak before the Board of Education on the math that was taught.

They met offsite, in the cafeteria of a nearby school. Board members, the district superintendent, and select teachers were in attendance. He told them of the above teaching method, which was approved with great appeal.


Visual Discernment

Sometimes Mr. Nanni would put a math problem on the board, and purposely write something that was incorrect. He would wait for one of the students to see his error and correct him. He called that "visual discernment," as he wanted his students to catch his error.

When they did, he would say, "Good for you! Sometimes people make mistakes, and I want you to be able to catch them."

Listening Skills

In teaching most lessons, he kept his students attentive with his comical antics. He was teaching listening skills, discernment, and creativity all at the same time. His class had to stay alert to keep up with him. He would say:

> Jack and Jill
> went up the hill,
> and fell over the
> candlestick.

Or,

Humpty Dumpty
sat on a wall,
Humpty Dumpty
had a great fall.
All the king's horses,
and all the king's men,
lived in a shoe and
didn't know what to do.

Or,

Little Miss Muffet,
sat on a tuffet,
eating her curds and
whey.  Along came
Goosey Gander and
squashed the spider
away.

In each instance, he would wait in amusement for the students to correct him and tell him how the nursery rhyme really should be said. He took great pleasure in hearing sixth grade students recite children's nursery rhymes!

A colleague of his, Joel Pehote, said that he played mind games with the students. However, his methods kept his students always looking forward to his classes.

Inspiring Students

When Mr. Nanni entered a new class, he would tell them, "I look at you and I see how much you can learn, and what you can be. Why you could be the next President, or a doctor, or the best scientist in the world." He always wanted them to be inspired to be the best that they could be.

If Mr. Nanni found that some of his students looked particularly sleepy or disinterested, he would say to his class, "There is something in this room different from yesterday. Whoever finds it gets an extra point. You have one minute to find it and write it down on a piece of paper."

It could be something moved closer to the window, no eraser on the chalk board, a new lesson on the board, or an instruction to read. The students would always perk up to find the changed item.

## Following Directions

Mr. Nanni would stand in the back of the room where the students couldn't watch him as he gave directions.

"Take out a plain piece of loose-leaf paper and place it on your desk lengthwise, with the top of the sheet toward the front of the class."

"Next," he would tell them, "place your right hand index finger on the lower left-hand corner of the sheet, and your left hand on the upper right side of the sheet.

"Now, place the upper right-hand corner on the bottom left-hand corner and fold the sheet, holding onto the corner with your left hand.

"Then, take your right hand and put your index finger on the bottom right-hand corner, and fold the paper up until the corner meets the left-hand top corner, and fold the sheet."

Whatever shape the paper came out to be, he would check to see that they followed his directions.

## Dictionary Game

In his teaching days, a dictionary was provided on each desk. Today, there may be an electronic device in its place to do the exercise.

As was typical, his lessons were usually made into games, and were designed to challenge an opposing team.

The students were put into teams by row. A word, such as "limousine" was given to them. Each student had to find the word in the dictionary. As the word was found, they were to raise their hand.

The first complete row to find the word was selected, and Mr. Nanni would pick any one of the students in that row to close the dictionary and tell what the word meant in their own words.


Eraser Tag

Just for the diversion, as done in many classrooms, Mr. Nanni would let his students play eraser tag. Rules were explained, and one girl and one boy were chosen to balance a blackboard eraser on their heads. Based on the starting direction, either party was to catch up with the other and tag them "out."

If the eraser fell off of one of their heads, they were "out," and another person was chosen. As the race went on, Mr. Nanni would change the direction from "boy chase girl," or "girl chase boy," throughout the game.

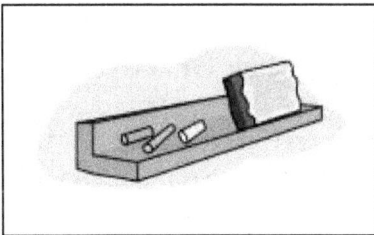

Blackboard Eraser

If there was a lesson in this game, it was sportsmanship, but listening and following directions certainly played a role.

## Stimulating Creativity

Mr. Nanni was great about getting his students to rally around an idea that he would present. The students would raise their hands when they had a question or something to add to his original theme. This would then evoke stimulating conversation among the group.

He might ask, "If you were really sick and needed a doctor, would you pick one that graduated with a test score of 70% or 100%?"

Or, he might ask, "If you decide not to go on to further your education, what would you do to support yourself and maybe your family?"

Each question would stimulate comments, and the open conversations would kindle further ideas. This exercise would also encourage the ability for full class participation.

## Field Trips

Knowing that there is a lot to learn on a field trip, Mr. Nanni wanted to have an overnight outing at a camp for his 6th grade class. One of the other teachers, Joe Doran, was also excited about the idea, but wanted to plan a whole week camping trip. It had to be approved by the Board of Education, and it was.

Mr. Doran actually took the lead and was at the head of organizing this venture. He had been very involved with a foundation called De Colores, meaning "the colors."

---

Mr. Nanni was unsuccessful in reaching Mr. Doran for more than two years prior to this printing, but it was felt important to credit him for his work.

This foundation, which began in Tijuana, Mexico, is a non-profit organization that focuses on helping developmentally challenged children. Additionally, their charter includes a segment against domestic violence, as it pertains to women and children.

"De Colores" is also a traditional folk song that is well known throughout the Spanish-speaking world. Its origin is unknown; however, it is believed to have been in circulation since the 16th century.

The one-week camping trip was held at a facility of a Catholic Youth Organization in Port Sanilac, Michigan. Joe Doran was Camp Director there, so it was fitting that he also partake in directing some of the activities.

All of the 6<sup>th</sup> grade class and teachers were involved, as well as other leaders and chaperones.

The attendees learned about nature, compass reading, predators and prey. Some of their activities included, but were not limited to, a treasure hunt, archery, tie dying, and other arts and crafts.

The head organizer modeled the week's activities after the programs at De Colores. Later, Mr. Nanni became involved in the activities of the foundation.

Leadership

Many of the group activities required a team leader. Following military style, Mr. Nanni would say, "I want the best commander," who was readily picked out by the group.

He then began teaching leadership to the sixth graders. He explained what the commander was to do, and how the others were to follow his authority.

## Discipline

Not totally serious, but stern enough, Mr. Nanni kept a strict camp. He had cabin inspection, and used a white glove test for dust! This was a lesson in discipline, and afterwards, he would give an award to the best kept cabin.

## Trust

The kids also participated in an exercise in trust that was later done in large corporations. The leader would have some of the kids stand on a picnic table, one at a time, and the others were to hold hands to form a net around the table.

The one standing on the table would do a deliberate free fall, and the students holding hands would have to catch that person. That was to teach them both teamwork and trust.

## Team Work

Other fun activities for sport included both boys and girls running track. The boys competed against boys, and the girls against girls. Their times were recorded and they vied to see who would win the race.

One of the girl runners twisted her ankle during a run. Her parents were called, and she was taken to the hospital.

Still, after a cast was put on, she refused to go home. She insisted on staying at camp and was determined to participate in the race. She couldn't run, but she made her way around the track in crutches just to be included in the sport.

## Map Drawing

One of the more educational assignments was to have the students make a map of their current area. They had to plot out both distance and direction from a center point, drawing buildings, trees, a stump, bike rack, and so on.

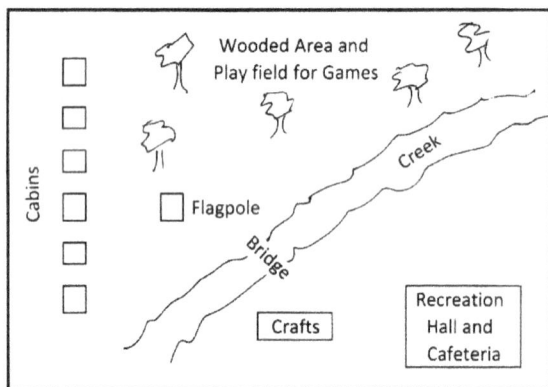

Campground

Measurements were made by pacing off. One pace would equal about three feet, depending on their height.

They also had to determine the distance across the stream by use of geometry-based triangulation.

In this case, the distance was estimated by pacing off a set number of paces sideways and backwards, and then forming a triangle, thereby judging the width of the stream.

Other Fun

Another activity, especially enjoyed by the boys, was a slide down a steep hill to Sucker's Creek.

Wikipedia: Triangulation is the process of determining the location of a point by measuring angles to it from known points at either end of a fixed baseline. The point can then be fixed as the third point of a triangle with one known side and two known angles.

There was a ravine on the hill, which had a drop off, and if you hit it, you were sure to go in the creek. The small stream got its name, Sucker's Creek, from those who went down the hill and landed in the water.

There was also a tree with a rope hanging down and a knot at the end, and the challenge was to swing across the creek without falling in. Of course, the boys liked falling in just as well as not. The creek was only knee deep.

To make it more interesting, the leaders created a story about a huge rock in the creek that was submerged just below the waterline.

It was barely visible, and they told the kids that Frankenstein was buried there. They all wanted to see Frankenstein's grave, and some climbed the embedded rock.

The stream provided more excitement, as it had a single rope bridge with side ropes that spanned across the water. The kids had to hold onto the side ropes to make it across the bridge safely.

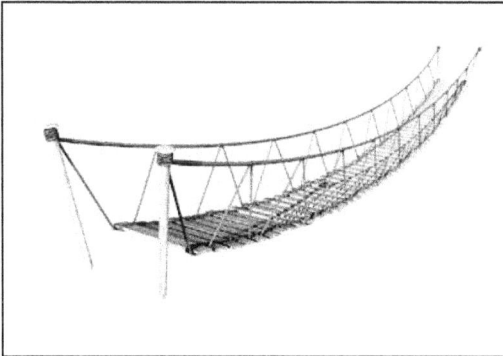

Rope Bridge

The week was filled with events, and another game was created called "Capture the Flag." The group was divided into two teams, one having a red flag and the other a green one.

A person from each team was the protector of their flag. Members of the opposite team could do any number of things to divert the attention away from the protector, so that the flag could be captured and taken a distance away.

Examples of diversion might be dancing, jumping up and down, wrestling, singing, or joke telling.

They also played "Capture the Camper," where the students could hide somewhere on the grounds, and the counselors had to find them. They students were not allowed to go into any of the buildings on the site.

Not at all fair to the sixth graders, but when they played "Capture the

Counselor," the counselors hid inside the buildings!

There was only one student who had to be sent home for being disorderly. He broke all of the rules, and was not a team player. His father was called to come and get him, and he was dismissed.

# Interactive Studies

<u>Twenty Questions</u>

This exercise would stimulate thinking and be fun for the students. Mr. Nanni would say, "I have an object in my pocket, and you are to ask me questions about what the object might be."

He explained to them, "I can only answer 'yes' or 'no,' so ask me any question that might even seem dumb, like is it paper, plastic, rubber, etc."

By process of elimination, the object was narrowed down. If he said 'yes,' there would be countless possibilities, and it would make them think.

## Deductive Reasoning

Sometimes he would change the game as follows. "I'm thinking of something that is an object. You can ask me, 'Is it smaller than a bread box?,' or 'is it bigger than a bicycle?'

"If I say 'yes,' you should keep asking questions until you guess what the object is. These are questions to get to the truth of what the object is.

"This is deductive reasoning," he would say, "forming a conclusion from a set of statements."

## Inductive Reasoning

Another type of reasoning is inductive reasoning. "You cannot ask, 'Is it a dog?' That's making a direct statement, and not using reasoning. You might ask,

'Does the object have legs?'
That's inductive reasoning.''

Or, he might say, "I'm
looking for an object that was
once part of a tree." Each
exercise would engage the
whole class and get them
thinking, and, it would be
fun.


Cause and Effect

Along with his training
responsibility, students were
taught to appreciate the cause
and effect for their actions.
One of his favorite examples
by Ben Franklin follows:


For the want of a nail
the shoe was lost.

For the want of a shoe
the horse was lost.

For the want of a horse
the rider was lost.

For the want of a rider
the battle was lost.

For the want of a battle
the kingdom was lost.

And all for the want of
a horseshoe-nail.

Prime cause: all because of a
nail.

There are many variations to
this old saying, but the
meaning is still the same: the
cause of one thing affects
another.

Mr. Nanni also used this
example for a writing assignment or verbal discussion,
where the student had to
describe an action, and
analyze the consequences of
the event or decision.

## Recognizing Emotions

Emotional competency was also felt to be important. Being able to recognize, interpret, and respond constructively to others was shown to be valuable, but to also recognize their own emotions in a situation was equally important.

In his creative mind, Mr. Nanni would pose questions to his students. He would ask, "What is the worst thing that could ever happen to you?"

Most students would answer *to die*, and he would ask, "Would you pass on to oblivion?"

Then he would ask what "oblivion" meant. Some of the students would try to define the word, but he would explain that it meant a state of being completely forgotten or unknown.

Then he would ask, "Do you want me to remember you?"

"Of course," the students said.

Then he would ask, "Do you want me to care about you?"

Of course, they did. He would then explain that their actions would determine whether someone would care about them. He taught that it was important to be remembered by the nice person that they were and the thoughtful things that they did.

This lesson taught the importance of behavior, not only of themselves, but of those around them.

# Subject Oriented Teachings

## Spelling Test

Always keeping the students alert, the first question on the test was, "What was the name of this spelling unit?" The students would have to answer, "Learning how to use Adjectives" in order to get credit.

The rest of the test included qualified words that must be spelled correctly.

## Sentence Diagramming

He also believed in students having to diagram sentences, as he felt it made the lessons of parts of speech and their usage more meaningful to them.

A simple example:

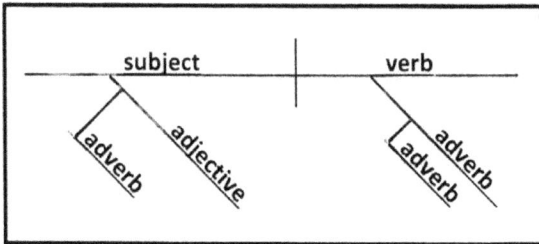

Or, more complex diagram-ming:

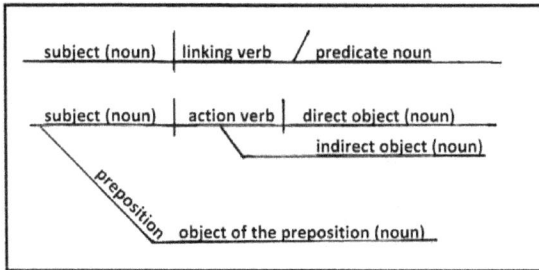

Sentence examples:

1. The grey fox jumped over the fence.

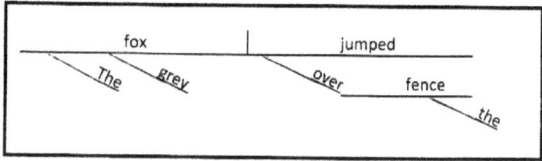

The grey fox jumped over the fence.

2. A thin layer of dust covered the coffee table in the living room.

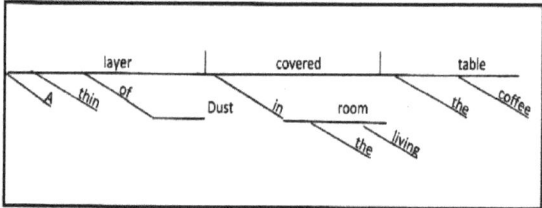

## Essay Writing

Topics were given that would make students use their creative abilities and get them to think. They were encouraged to write about conflicting ideas, or issues of adventure or survival, using their personal views.

Assignments would be to write an essay using topics such as:

> Man vs. Self
> Good vs. Evil
> Man against Nature
> Man against Wilderness

When an assignment was given, Mr. Nanni didn't mind if the answer was incorrect, just so that it was backed up by logic. If there was a good argument for the statements made, he would give credit.


## Story Starters

As part of teaching English, literature, and independent writing, students had to complete sentences that were put on the board.

For example:

> You were walking late at night. All of a sudden . . .

Or,

> What in the world happened to . . .

Or,

> Suddenly, there was a loud . . .

For example, on the above sentence starter, they were taught to use descriptive words such as bang, noise, scream.

Sometimes he would call on a student in the classroom to add to his story. He might say, "One day, three boys were. . ." and the student called upon would have to complete the sentence.

The next person called upon would have to add to the story with an open-ended statement, and the next person would have to finish it. This would continue until an entire story was created.

Another exercise of creative writing that his students enjoyed was this.

He would say, "You all know the stories with Larry, Curly, and Moe. Now write a story of what happens when Larry, Curly, and Moe meet up with Popeye."

Or, the assignment could be meeting up with Little Miss Muffet, or even Humpty Dumpty. These exercises proved to be fun and creatively stimulating for the students.

To his astonishment, after giving a creative writing assignment, one of his most boisterous students surprised him. He never appeared to be interested in class, but wrote the most beautiful paper. It began with the sentence as shown.

"Grandfather sun reached down and kissed the tiny blades of grass . . ."

Mr. Nanni called it "awakening the talent within."

Poetry

A similar type of exercise, like story starters, was given for poetry. A poem was started on the board, and students would have to find rhyming words and compose a poem using those words.

He would also have his students show the degree of emphasis given a sound or syllable in speech. He used stress marks to show the canter, or rhythm in poetry.

He would explain that accented syllables are pronounced slightly louder and with a higher pitch than unaccented syllables.

He used the following example to show the rhythm in poetry:

> 'Twas the night before Christmas
> And all though the house
> Not a creature was stirring
> Not even a mouse

He would also tell them, "Poetry is important. You could get a job writing poetry, maybe with a card company like Hallmark. Think of all the beautiful verses there are on the cards that you receive. Someone has to write them."

He also wanted to impress upon them how important it was to learn English. "Do you want to know why you have to learn English? Have you ever written a letter?

---

'Twas the Night Before Christmas was published anonymously in 1823 and later attributed to Clement Clarke Moore, who claimed authorship in 1837.

"How could you express exactly what you want to tell the other person if you can't write it well? You need it to write poetry, too. English reflects on you and what you know."

## Handwriting

The Common Core standards, as they are known, don't require cursive reading or writing in many states today. It has been replaced by learning the keyboard and computers. Many tests are now taken on computers.

Although there is little emphasis on cursive handwriting today, some educators feel it is a great loss to students' learning. The lack of this teaching has been called a "casualty of progress." I, too, feel it is a great travesty.

Nevertheless, in his class-room, Mr. Nanni stressed the importance of penmanship. He wanted his students to relax the hand, and to write with the hand, and not the fingers.

He taught them to use discipline when writing. He had sheets of lined paper made up so that his students could take a full class period to make sure their letters all slanted the same way.

Another day they were to work on the size of the letters and to stay inside the lines.

He would also make lines on the blackboard, two fingers apart, and show an example of correct lettering. Students were to write on their lined paper all letters that began at the line with an over stroke, like "a, c, and d" and practice writing them.

They were then instructed to write those letters that began with an under curve, like "i, e, and f," and to practice them. They must all be slanted the same way, and this was to be done without over writing the letters below them.

www.handwriting.pk

Permission of this example was given by Jamal Muhsin, an author and instructor of penmenship and calligraphy in Pakistan.

To emphasize the importance of legible handwriting, Mr. Nanni would scribble their homework assignment on the board in a way that no one could read it.

"I can't read that," he heard from many students in the class.

"Well sometimes I can't read your writing either!" he would say.

He stressed that handwriting reflects who you are, so if you don't want to be regarded as sloppy, don't use sloppy handwriting.

In regard to homework, he would tell his students that the hardest thing is getting started. The best time to do homework is right away when you get home. Do it when everything is fresh in your mind, not later when you're tired.

## Left-handed Writers

Mr. Nanni wrote with his left hand, and he learned to write with the proper slant from a Nun in primary school. She just adjusted the slant of the paper so that the writing was correct. He was grateful to her for that teaching, and he passed that knowledge on to his left-handed writers.

One of his students, Daniel Trotta, recalled that Mr. Nanni was left handed, and had the most beautiful penmanship. "It inspired me to develop mine. In fact, he could write better with his right hand than most right-handed folks!"

He also remembered that Mr. Nanni was always impeccably dressed. "I remember his wing tip shoes and finely pressed clothes."

He also went on to say, "We have many teachers

throughout life. Many we do not remember, and then there are those we never forget. Mr. Nanni is one I have never forgotten over the last 46 years. He inspired me to be a top performer in life, not by what he said, but by his actions. He truly cared about his students and was a great teacher, motivator and human being."

## Using Adverbs and Adjectives

An old, but popular cigarette commercial, "Winston tastes good like a cigarette should," was stated to his students, and he would ask what part of speech "good" was.

It was important to him to recognize the improper usage in the advertising. He would then teach that good was an adjective describing a noun; and well was an adverb modifying a verb.

Further, he would say, "I'm feeling very well," not good. He taught the difference between "the good boy" and "the well boy." He used this example: "The good boy has done his work very well."

He also noted the musical notes that were to be remembered by the acronym EGBDF, Every Good Boy Does Fine, noting that it should be "every good boy does well."

Reading

Not new to education, but the school would have a contest to see who could read the most books in a certain timeframe.

The competition was usually between all of the classrooms in the school. The numbers were tallied up, and a recognition award was given to the classroom with the

56

highest number of books read.

While it was agreed that this was a great endeavor to encourage reading, Mr. Nanni didn't put as much emphasis in this effort as he did his own methods. He preferred to teach speed reading and comprehension in his own manner.

## Speed Reading

He taught that speed reading required taking note of the first and last sentence, and then summing up what was said in the paragraph.

He trained his students to ask themselves the meaning of the paragraph, and to write a statement as a note for their own reference.

He told his class that John Kennedy could read 2,000 words a minute. Most kids learned to read 200 to 400 words a minute, but one of his students almost made it to 2,000.

John Kennedy's secret was this. Don't look at each word. Look at a group of words, as your eye will see them and read them.

Instead of using a cover card under each line of type as you read, Mr. Nanni also taught to place it above the line that you are reading so that you can read the lines underneath more quickly.

Another student, Tony Trotta, recalls Mr. Nanni teaching the class speed reading using the Readers Digest. He said, "We were to note the main points and thereby improve our overall reading skills."

## Comprehension

After learning how to do speed reading, Mr. Nanni would say, "Now that you have learned to read quickly, think about what you have read and write it down."

There were no shortcuts to his teachings. The student always had to fully understand the reasons for his lessons and be ready to react with the right response or directive.

## Math

Math was also taught in extraordinary ways. Mr. Nanni would do an exercise he called Rapid Fire Math.

The students were to write the numbers 1 through 10 on the lines of a sheet of paper.

He would then give ten multiplication table questions

very quickly: 10 x 7, 7 x 6, 9 x 5, 4 x 6, 8 x 9, 3 x 9, etc., and the students would have to write the answers to each multiplication table as fast as they could.

He would also use flash cards with written questions or multiplication tables on them.

To keep it interesting, sometimes he would have a student say, "I want to challenge (any student in the room by name) to answer the problem on this card."

In that way, every student had to stay alert and attentive.

Mr. Nanni also talked to his students about math and the value of money. "You're 11 or 12 years old now. You know, you could be a millionaire by the time you're 40.

Do you get an allowance?"
Most of the kids would raise
their hands.

"If you put ½ of your
allowance in the bank, that
money would accrue interest.
It would also compound,
which means that you would
also earn interest on the
interest you just earned.

"Or, when you get a job, put
$50 a week away. Learn to
start saving money. That's a
very important lesson in
life!"

Some of his math exercises
were taught in very practical
ways. "Why do you need to
know math?" he would ask.

"Let's say you want to carpet
a room. You will need to
measure both the length and
width of the room to know
how much carpeting to buy.

"Or, you want to paint a
room that is 12 by 14 feet,

and the walls are 8 feet high. You find that a gallon of paint will cover 100 sq. ft. with 2 coats. You must figure w x l x h (width times length times height) to figure how many gallons of paint to buy.

"The value of math is in how to use it for what you need."

In teaching fractions, using this example,

$$
\begin{array}{r}
4\text{-}1/2 \\
-\ \underline{2\text{-}7/8} \\
\end{array}
$$

he would ask, "What multiplication process do you need to do to the denominator and to the numerator?"

He would explain that it was
necessary to make the ½ into
8ths by multiplying it by 4,
making it 4/8ths.

```
        4-4/8
    —   2-7/8
```

"How can you subtract 7/8
from 4/8?" Keeping in story
form, he would say, "You
must knock on the door of the
4 and borrow 1 to add 8 8ths
to the 4 8ths, making it 12
8ths."

Now you have this:

```
        3
        4̸-12/8
    —   2- 7/8
```

Now it is easy to subtract,
and the answer is 1-5/8.

In teaching geometry, he would begin by saying that a circle has 360°. If you draw a straight line through it, you have 180° on each side.

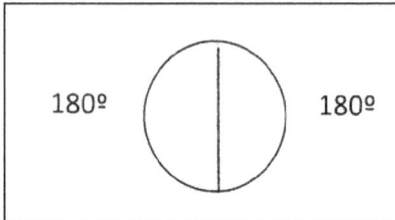

Every triangle, big or small, has a total of 180°. If you draw a straight line through it you have 90° angles on the inside. If the sides are equal, you have an equilateral triangle.

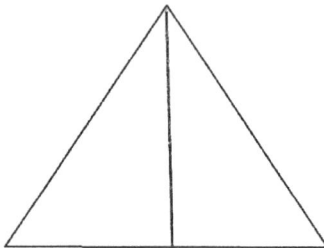

The angles of each corner are 60°, as shown.

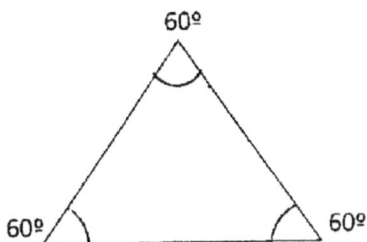

If you draw a perpendicular line through the triangle and split it in two, you have all of these angles.

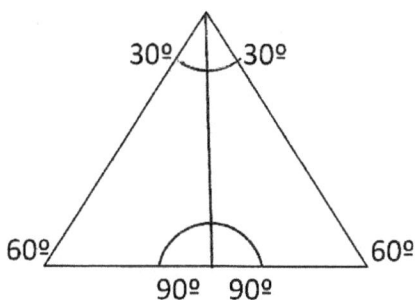

He stressed, "It doesn't do any good to learn these skills if you can't do things around the house with them."

Another day he would take the class outside on the lawn and tell them to form groups and find a place to work. He gave them strings and told them to go find a stick, and make a loose loop at one end of the string so that the stick can go through it. He also gave them long pieces of rope.

By putting the stick in the ground, and stretching the string out, they were to make a circle, putting the rope in place to form the circle.

He would then go from group to group with a measuring tape and have them measure the circle's circumference.

He would also have them find the radius, which is drawn from the center to the circumference. He showed them that when making the circle smaller, the radius is less.

Other times, a playground having loose dirt was used to make the circle, and the rope was unnecessary.

To him, this lesson was teaching practical math, and the basis for learning how to use a compass.

Some exercises he used to develop math skills were to have the students write the numbers 1 through 10 on the left side of the paper, leaving room between each number.

He would say, "Using your pencil and eraser, transpose the numbers 5 and 8. Now transpose the numbers 1 and 10, reversing their position."

Or, he would ask, "Can you count from 1 to 30? Let me hear you count backwards from 30 to 2, skipping every other number. Now forward from 1 to 29 skipping every other number. Now start with 32 and count backwards by 4."

Mr. Nanni was asked to be a math tutor for one of his female students. Among his other exercises, he would have the girl counting backwards from 100 to 1, then skipping numbers, and doing only even or only odd numbers both forward and backward as above.

The girl later became an engineer, and he was so proud of her!

## Competition Between Classrooms

Working in teams to solve problems became common-place in Mr. Nanni's classroom. He and his colleague, Bill Stanz, who was teaching in the next room, worked together to make the exercises more challenging.

There happened to be a hole in the wall between the rooms to add some interest. You might surmise that the teachers had as much fun as the students.

Each of the classrooms were given challenges in math or English, and competed against one another to be the winning team.

Of course, the exchange of information through the hole in the wall made the competition more intriguing.

With the aid of another colleague, Joel Pehote, Mr. Nanni created another way to conduct competition between classrooms.

He bought an inexpensive portable intercom system,

and hooked it up between Mr. Pehote's classroom and his. Each class had been taught Social Studies lessons about our North American neighbors, such as Canada, Mexico, and South America.

With the use of the intercom system, one class would challenge the other class to answer questions about those continents.

Mr. Nanni loved challenges. One year he asked his class, "How would you like to win the Campbell Soup Label contest?" The class was quite receptive.

"This is how you do it," he explained. "Go to all of the homes near where you live, or anywhere you visit, and collect all that you can. Form groups of 2 or 3, if you like, and go door-to-door. Remember not to talk about what you collect to anyone outside of this classroom."

All of the labels collected from his class weren't turned in until the very last day! They won the contest.

# Extraneous Teachings

<u>Outlining</u>

Mr. Nanni taught his students to take notes in outline form, and to use them on a test. An example of outlining follows:

```
I. Main Idea
    A. Supporting Idea
        1. Subset of A
        2. Subset of B
            a) Subset of 2
            b) Subset of 2

II. Second Main Idea
    A. Supporting Idea
```

Continuing his ability to teach a full mix of skills in very practical ways, he would instruct them as follows:

"When the bell rings and you hear the PA announcements, begin outlining what is said, complete with Roman numerals, capital letters, numbers and small letters."

The subjects might include something about the lunch hour behavior, recess, a parent-teacher conference, etc.

He encouraged them to learn to outline, and to use their notes when studying for a test.


Test Taking

Many students freeze up when taking a test and cannot think clearly. When giving a test, he told his students to begin with the easiest questions, and warm up to the more difficult ones.

Sometimes Mr. Nanni would give a test, and surprise his

students by saying, "You can check your own papers." Suddenly there would be a look of awe on their faces.

"When we're done, I want you to state on the bottom of the sheet, 'This paper was checked by a very honest person.' Then sign your name."

He would then say, "Now, exchange papers with someone else in the class. The last person in each row should bring the papers up to the front." He continually made his students listen and follow directions.

Other times, he would write on the top of the test, "READ ENTIRE TEST OVER. ONLY SIGN YOUR NAME TO THIS PAPER." He always wanted to be sure his students were kept alert, following directions, and thinking.

## Health and the Dangers of Smoking

The students were given a study unit on health, and were shown a movie on the dangers of smoking.

They were told that people who smoke or use tobacco are at risk of developing cancer of the throat or larynx.

They were shown that the larynx is located in the throat and that it houses the voice box.

"If you have to have your larynx removed, you will lose your voice," he stated. In the movie they were told that their voice would no longer be normal and were able to hear how it would sound.

Mr. Nanni told them, "You will have a hole put in your neck and have a tube inserted so that you can breathe, and a voice box to help you speak."

Not satisfied that the movie had made a strong enough impression, he did a demonstration on smoking.

He brought a blood pressure cuff into the classroom, and had the students check his blood pressure. It was something like 120/80.

He then lit up a cigarette in the classroom, and the students immediately reacted and said, "You can't smoke in here."

He jokingly replied that he wasn't smoking, the cigarette was--but he wanted to demonstrate what damage smoking actually did.

After taking a puff of a cigarette, his blood pressure was taken again, and it was higher. He also had a couple of his students check his pulse before and after.

Not being a smoker, Mr. Nanni did some choking and sputtering to do the exercise. He took a handkerchief out of his pocket, and then a puff of the cigarette. With a mouth full of smoke, he put the handkerchief up to his mouth and blew the smoke out.

A brown spot appeared on the cloth, and the kids said, "Ooooh!" They didn't like the looks of it.

Then he took another puff, and this time inhaled. It actually made him dizzy, as he blew smoke into the handkerchief right next to the last spot. It was a little lighter in color.

"Why do you suppose it's lighter now?" he asked. "The rest of it went into my lungs." He also told them that this test with a filtered cigarette was not much different.

"Do you know how to tell who is a smoker?" he asked. "Look at their fingers. They're all yellow."

Many of the students inspected their fingers. They had probably tried smoking. Mr. Nanni hardly left a trick untold.

"Besides that," he said, "you'll have bad breath if you smoke."

## Hygiene

Sometimes Mr. Nanni would begin his class saying, "Put your hair behind your ears and your hands flat on your desk." He would then walk around the room checking each student for clean nails and if they had washed behind their ears.

He stressed the importance of good hygiene, and some students who weren't too sure if their nails were clean would hide their hands under their desk!

## Speed of Light

Mr. Nanni kept fun and games in his lessons. When teaching about the speed of light, he certainly taught the facts, but he kept his students amused by having them partake in the exercises.

To teach about the speed of light, he would go to the light switch on the wall, and turn it off and on. When he turned it off, he would ask his students, "Where did the light go? It had to go somewhere.

"Light travels at 186,000 miles per second. That's like 15 or 16 times around the world!," he would say. He also taught that it would take 24,906 miles to go around the world.

There was an empty storage closet in the classroom that was at least five feet wide. He picked out one of his more congenial students, and told him to get in the closet.

"Do you see any light in there?" he asked.

"Yes, I see cracks of light around the door," was the answer.

He then proceeded to duct tape the cracks of the door from the outside.

"Do you see any light in there now?" he asked again.

"No, no light," said the student.

"Then come out of the closet," instructed Mr. Nanni.

The student tried to get out, but, of course, it was sealed shut with tape.

"I can't get out," came the voice from inside.

"Then get way back and get a running start," he was told.

The laughter in the classroom was almost uncontrollable, as the student burst through the ripped tape and came flying through the opened door.

This wouldn't be allowed in today's teaching environment, but it was one of the classroom's most memorable days.

Although the principal of the school reprimanded him from time to time, there was a mutual understanding and admiration between them. Mr. Nanni respected the principal as the best he ever had, and the principal respected Mr. Nanni for his teaching abilities.

A few years back, he saw that student while shopping in a

music store, and they recounted the memory of his being closed up in the closet. It was still remembered as an amusing and harmless experience.

Because Mr. Nanni was so unconventional, he made learning both entertaining and memorable. The students were exceedingly attentive to all of the lessons taught in his classroom.


## Mind Warm-Up Exercise

He explained to his students that athletes warm up with exercise, so why not warm up your mind?

They were told to put their heads down on their desks, and empty their minds until they saw total blackness.

They were then instructed to change the darkness to be totally white.

Now, put a black dot right in the middle of the white background. They were to raise their hands when they saw the black dot.

Now, change the black dot to green. Again, students would raise their hands.

Now, around the green dot, put a square.

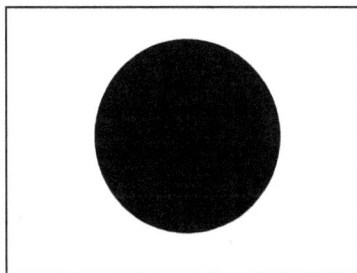

In this way, he taught mind readiness and concentration. His students never knew what to expect in his classroom.

## Drama with Hand Puppets

This exercise was not only to encourage drama, it was a way to allow students to use their creativity.

They were instructed to bring in a pair of socks from home. In the classroom, they created faces and appropriate dress for the puppets with markers, paints, and other available materials.

They were told that they would need to have one puppet teach the other one a lesson, and to present the lesson in front of the class.

The lesson could be how to tie a shoe, wash a window, weave a basket, change a flat tire, or how to spell a word. While one puppet was teaching the other, the student would have to change their voice for the respective puppet.

Example:

Puppet 1: How do you spell algebra?

Puppet 2: Algebra?

Puppet 1: Yes, algebra. How do you spell it?

Puppet 2: A-l-g-e-b-r-a

This exercise also taught them to loosen up in a fun way and enabled them to be less inhibited when speaking in front of a group.

## Spontaneous Public Speaking

Extemporaneous speaking was found to be a great way to get students to express themselves in front of other students. He felt that eventually, public speaking would come naturally to them.

Students would have one minute to think about what they were going to say about a given topic.

It might be, "What do you know about football?" Or he might ask another student, "Describe what it is like to weave a basket."

Sometimes students were given a problem:

Your neighbor is a boy who always picks fights, but the boy is your best friend. What do you tell him?

Or, another dilemma might be:

Your best friend is cheating on a test. What do you say to him?

Mr. Nanni credits some of his inspiration from a book for drama students called *Can of Squirms*, which included a Leader Guide to help with facilitation.

This book included "role-playing games of fun and discovery, and presented intellectually stimulating ideas to teach young people the benefits of moral and ethical responsibility."

---

Book of Squirms: Meriwether Publishing, Downers Grove, Ill.: Contemporary Drama Service, Arthur Meriwether inc., 1969-1971.

Giving praise to his teaching methods, one of Mr. Nanni's students wanted to be a singer. However, he didn't have the courage to sing in front of an audience.

After he experienced the teaching techniques of Mr. Nanni, he was able to sing "The Wind Beneath My Wings" in front of the class.

## Strengths and Weaknesses

After a lengthy teaching session, Mr. Nanni would ask his students to write on a piece of paper what they had just learned and turn it in. He could then assess what impressions the lesson had made on them.

As mentioned earlier, Mr. Nanni's daughter, Angela, is a teacher. She teaches $9^{th}$ through $12^{th}$ grades, although earlier in her career she taught younger aged students.

Recently, about half way through the semester, she asked her students to write a paper telling what they thought their strengths were, and another, to assess their weaknesses.

She stressed that they should also tell what they were most proud of. "Even if you only got one question right on a difficult math test, you should be proud that you got one right!"

She felt that this self analysis could help her understand each student better, but also make them tap into their inner strength.

She told her students that one's greatest weakness is to give up. She wanted to be sure that each student set a goal to improve their weakness, and then she could help them to do better.

This exercise also gave the students a sense of ownership and responsibility.

Mr. Nanni stated that if he were to go back to teaching, he would find at least one complementary thing about each student and praise them. "It is so important to build self esteem in those young people," he said.

Word Exercises

Mr. Nanni would write a word on the board. He would then ask his students:

What is the definition?

Now, what is the synonym?

And the antonym?

Now use the word correctly in a sentence.

Now tell me, what is a word that rhymes with this word?

Playful as he was, he would say, "What is the cinnamon?," and wait for his students to correct him.

# The Amazon
# Rain Forest Trip

## A Class Project

A history lesson was given about the Brazilian Rain Forest in South America. The students were told about the climate, terrain and culture of this picturesque area. Mr. Nanni had a projector, and showed many visuals on a screen, which were taken from National Geographic.

Amazon Rain Forest

He asked his class, "How would you like to take a trip to this Rain Forest?" Eyes would open wide in wonderment, as he explained further.

"Well, I'll have to see if I can get a helicopter to fly you in there," he said. "The only one I know who would fly you there is this ape," and he held up a stuffed animal complete with hat and goggles.

The students laughed. "The only problem is," he went on, "he doesn't know how to land. You'll have to use a parachute, and many dangers await you!"

The students were told to bring in any material, such as fabric, part of a sheet, plastic, or a handkerchief that would make a parachute. They should also bring some kind of a weight like a nut, bolt, or fishing line sinker.

The next day in class, the students made parachutes. As part of their learning experience, they were taken outside where they could throw them up in the air. When they got caught in a tree, he warned, "That's what could happen to you!"

He also taught them how to read a compass while they were outdoors.

The class spent the entire month working on this creative class participation project. It taught many things to the students, including science, the study of animals, fish, cultures, budgets, finance, survival, writing, communication, creativity, and the use of artistic skills.

Students worked in groups of three. Mr. Nanni created 100 "hazard cards." Students were given a set of rules before starting out on their trip. They could each carry a backpack of no more than 40 lbs. as the terrain was hazardous, and heavy loads would be too difficult to carry.

Each team had a budget of $1,000.00. They were told that they would be dropped by parachute, and many dangers awaited them. They could not carry guns, and they weren't allowed to kill anything.

Each day the team would pick up a new hazard card. Examples might be:

There are big crocodiles all around, with mouths

open wide.  How are you
going to escape them?

Crocodile

You've been attacked by
poisonous ants.  How are
you going to get rid of
them?

There is a wild goose
tracking you.  How are
you going to lose him?

There are headhunters in
the Amazon that eat
humans;    they    are
cannibals.  How will you
avoid them?

You've been captured by a hostile native tribe. How will you get away from them?

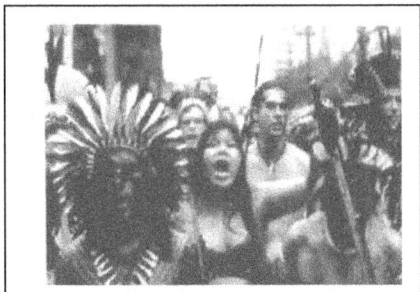

Hostile Native Tribe

An anaconda (giant snake) crawled into your tent. How will you get him out of there?

Some monkeys stole all of your food and your maps. How will you eat and find your way out of the forest?

One of your members is lost in the dark. How do you go about finding him?

Additional suggestions were given as follows:

They should take items with them that could be bartered. Common items to be traded were beads or jewelry, or even a mirror.

They could also take a camera to show the natives pictures of themselves.

Each student was to keep a journal of the challenges and solutions they faced every day, and write about them in their own words. They were graded at the end of the assignment on their diligence and ingenuity.

They also had to pick an independent topic about the rainforest to study, and to do research in order to write their findings in their journals. Examples might be about nature, culture, animal species, or plant life in the forest.

There are numerous animals in Africa, and many species of monkeys. One student reported on the Marmoset monkey from South America. Mr. Nanni admitted, "That proved to be a learning experience for the teacher!" They are about the size of a squirrel, and are constantly on the move searching for food.

The village houses were built on stilts and, at the end of the exercise, each group in the class had an assignment to build a replica of the village with houses out of paper or other available supplies.

Village Houses

This month-long project proved to be much more educational than following lessons from a book. Mr. Nanni suggests that other interesting projects might be the study of:

Greenland
Iceland
The Arctic and Bering Sea
Mount Everest in Asia

# Coaching Sports

During his teaching career, one of Mr. Nanni's colleagues, John Gretts, asked him to coach a wrestling team after school.

He had never taught the sport before, but found it to be an exceptional experience.

When I asked him how he liked teaching wresting, he said, "It's a great sport, and I have a philosophy about how to train kids to wrestle."

He taught them to be intense about the sport. He said that they should always be the aggressor and should use the same aggression in practice. They must also always be confident about their ability.

He also told them not to give their opponent any time to think.

"Intensity," he would say. "Don't let up."

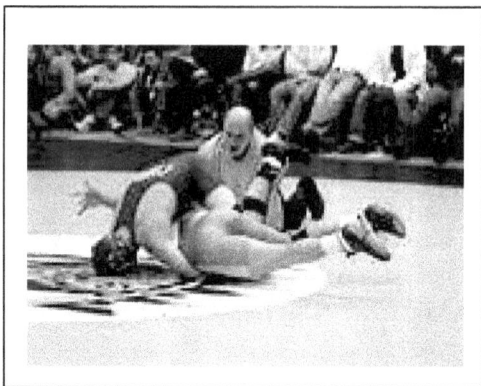

True to his word, he would set up a practice to go over the moves and instructed his students to be more intent and more aggressive.

He held "situation wrestling matches" with his students. He would say to them, "There are twenty seconds left to go, and you are down by 2 points. What are you going to do?"

Or, you're down on the mat with your opponent holding you down. How are you going to get out of that?

A wresting match had three periods of two minutes each. Even though these were 7th and 8th grade students, they played by high school rules.

As part of the practice, one wrestler would take the position on top, and the other would be on the floor.

1$^{st}$ period: Both wrestlers are standing.

- A point is scored by the wrestler who takes his opponent to the mat in full control.

- If the downed wrestler recovers to his feet, he is awarded an escape point.

- If the downed wrestler makes a reversal and gets control he is awarded two points.

2$^{nd}$ period: The referee throws a coin, and the color of the coin determines who gets the choice of where to start the period, on top, bottom, or neutral.

3$^{rd}$ period: If the match continues, the other wrestler gets his choice of top, bottom or neutral.

The referee is off to the side, leaning on one elbow, and when a wrestler is turned over, at least to a 45 degree angle, he starts counting.

Once that happens, and both shoulders touch the mat, a point is scored and that's the end of the match.

One of his students sent a letter to the high school principal stating that he learned so much about wrestling from Mr. Nanni that he went on to wrestle at Alma College.

Although Mr. Nanni put his whole heart into coaching wrestling, he enjoyed coaching football and basketball as well.

Two brothers, Tony and Daniel Trotta, had Mr. Nanni as their coach in basketball. Both of them remember being taught a two-hand chest pass, and that they could make half court shots that way as well.

Then there was Anthony, Mr. Nanni's "diamond in the rough" student, who made a statement about winners and losers in sports. He said, "If both teams play their best they are both winners, even if the score doesn't reflect it."

# Other Informative Teachings

## Disruptive Classroom

When the students got unruly and disruptive, Mr. Nanni found this to be a disservice to other students.

He claimed that yelling never works, so I found another way to keep them alert, listening, and learning.

He kept a non-working telephone on his desk. When the students got out of line, he would make a telephone call in front of the classroom.

"May I speak to Number One?"

(pause)

"Sure, I'll wait."

The kids would then listen attentively, to see what would be said.

"I have a problem. Well, you know. I don't know what to tell them."

(pause)

"Oh, all right, I'll let them know."

The kids would ask, "What did he say, what did he say?"

"He told me what would happen if you don't change your behavior. That's all I can tell you."

Even at their ages, and with a non-working telephone, the students became truly concerned about what could happen to them for misbehaving.

This tactic wouldn't be acceptable in today's teaching environment, but with his Catholic background, it worked for Mr. Nanni in his teaching days. Needless to say, he was always devoted to his faith.

Sometimes he would just ask the students to take out a sheet of paper. He would say, "Write a letter to your Mom or Dad and explain exactly what you were doing instead of learning. Take it home and have them sign it, and then bring it back to me. I don't want to have to do it, but if you don't write it, then I'll have to."

Another time when many of his students were unwilling to do their assigned work, he made a call to the principal's office and asked to have the school custodian come to his classroom.

When she did, he asked her to bring him a pail of water and a mop, and another pail of water with a squeegee.

She didn't ask any questions and, when she returned to the classroom with the requested supplies, he thanked her and closed his classroom door.

"Now," he told his students, "since you don't want to do the work I've assigned to you, you can do something to help the school out."

He pointed to a couple of troublemakers and told one of them to start mopping the floor, and the other to wash the windows.

## Conflict Resolution

Conflict Resolution was also taught by finding peaceful ways to resolve problems. His teachings follow.

Students were told that first you have to learn to respect the other person's feelings, and open up your mind to understanding their point of view.

They were taught that it was important to remain calm, and to act in a non-defensive way. Overreacting to a situation, or losing one's temper, will not result in resolving the conflict.

Understanding your own feelings in the dispute is also important. If you don't know why you feel the way you do, you won't be able to explain it to the other person.

Also, be sure to give positive, non-verbal signs to diffuse anger on the other side. Some of these are:

> Facial expressions
> Posture
> Gestures
> Tone of Voice

Introducing humor to a situation is also a positive addition to easing a conflict.

Most of all, remember that winning an argument is not always as important as keeping the relationship. Learn to make compromises and to forgive in order to resolve the conflict.

If the conflict cannot be resolved, accept that you disagree, and learn to let it go.

## Being Kind to Others

In his classroom, Mr. Nanni taught his students to be kind to one another, because you never knew what was on the other person's mind if they didn't respond to you well.

"Say you saw a student walking on the other side of the street and called out to them, but they didn't answer. They just kept walking with their head down. Maybe they had just been scolded by a parent or just weren't feeling well that day.

"Should you call him names? Embarrass him? You should learn to be more tolerant of people and accept that they have a reason for their behavior."

Next he took an 8-1/2" x 11" piece of paper and held it up in front of his students. He demonstrated in this way.

"Let's say you called that person a cruel name." Then Mr. Nanni tore a piece off of the corner of the paper. He continued the exercise by bullying the downtrodden student, and tearing another piece off from his paper example.

"You see," he said, showing the paper with missing pieces, "each time you offend the other person they lose something of themselves. Always be kind to others.

# Violence in the Classroom

Not all children were enthralled with Mr. Nanni's teachings. One student in particular was found making a drawing of a man being shot, another decapitated, and another mutilated. He saw these as thoughts of what the student felt about him.

Mr. Nanni asked him where he got such awful ideas. The youngster explained that he got them from a game he played at home. The parents were called, but gave no comment.

Mr. Nanni offered to give the student $20.00 for the game if he would bring it to school.

Upon receipt, Mr. Nanni gave the boy $20.00. He then smashed the game with a hammer, demonstrating violence in front of the classroom. He also explained to them what he thought about such a violent game and also his action of aggression.

He also explained that he was equally appalled by any display of brutality of animals in cartoons. He felt that there was a misconception in that form of exhibition, and any display of great cruelty instilled anger and hatred at the subconscious level.

Much discussion about violence followed. The students were encouraged to talk about the perils of violent behavior, and to tell stories of incidents they experienced or about which they knew.

A very good thing happened as a result of this unplanned exercise. The students became more aware of the violence to which they are exposed and how to avoid such encounters.

# Faith-Based Teachings

## Students Against Violence Everywhere (S.A.V.E.)

The students became so engaged in the subject matter of violence that they created an acronym to represent how they felt about that type of behavior. It was S.A.V.E., which stood for Students Against Violence Everywhere.

Mr. Nanni was so impressed with this creation that he registered the name with the Library of Congress.

As a token of appreciation, a sweatshirt was made for him by the class with S.A.V.E. across the front. It was signed by every student in the classroom and presented to him as a gift.

Mr. Nanni later formed a ministry with this name and carried this message on to all those with whom he came in contact. He believed that it was an important message to share with children and adults.

Students Against Violence Everywhere

## Angels Among Us

At that time, Mr. Nanni was acquainted with an equally spirited lady. She was also raised in a Catholic

117

environment, and they shared the desire to promote the teachings of a common good and well being for all.

She had spent fifteen years as part of the De Colores movement and worked with people in  the prison system in Detroit.  She worked with the inmates, and listened to the spiritual director tell the heartfelt story of the *Ragman*.

An entire program was developed, and twice a year members of De Colores stayed overnight at the prison, sleeping on mats on the gymnasium floor, to put on these programs.

After this involvement, ideas were copied from a presentation of "Angels Among Us" within the teachings of De Colores. These ideas were then developed into a childrens' version.

The program was brought to a youth home in Detroit, serving children whose ages ranged from 11 to 19.

It was apparent that these children had lost all self esteem and felt worthless. Through this program, they were taught that even though they had made mistakes, they were still valuable and could straighten themselves out.

Just like the lyrics of the song by many famed singers, they were taught to pick themselves up, dust themselves off, and start all over again. Much love was given to these children.

## Weekend Spiritual Group

A spiritual group of about twenty-five people was then formed, and a weekend program was developed, which was modeled after the teachings of De Colores. The program was created specifically for the youngsters in the group home of this Detroit correctional institution.

A facility with a kitchen and meeting room was located that was appropriate to host these weekend meetings, with the purpose of teaching children to feel closer to God.

Two presentations were developed and tailored for children. One was called the *Ragman*, which was taken from a book called the *Ragman and Other Cries of Faith*, by Walter Wangerin, Jr. The youngsters learned that God is everywhere and can be seen in the good deeds done by others.

---

Ragman and Other Cries of Faith, by Walter Wangerin, Jr.

The second presentation was from Martin Bell's short story, the *Barrington Bunny*, found in his book, *The Way of the Wolf*. It is an inspirational story about a lonesome bunny who thought he had nothing to offer.

Mr. Nanni created a CD of each story, complete with animated voices and music. His partner acted them out for the children.

The agenda began on a Thursday and taught much about love. The next day, the children were encouraged to talk about a personal situation where someone helped them to feel closer to God.

Later, the kids were asked to draw a picture of what they understood of the talk that was given.

---

Way of the Wolf, by Martin Bell

Some of the most touching moments were when a team member carried a cross into the meeting room and set it up among the children in attendance.

They were each given a nail and a piece of paper, and were instructed to write down something for which they wanted to be forgiven. They were then told to nail the paper to the cross.

When all had completed this task, the cross was then carried outside.

The papers, held by nails, were not looked at. They were burned on the cross outside. The meaning was that their sins were gone, and the burning was to represent the purity of forgiveness.

The cross was later returned to them inside in a renewed state. It might even be decorated with flowers or have other material draped over it. It was a very moving experience, where both the children and adults cried.

On Sunday, the closing day of the meeting, between 50 and 100 members would come in to hear the children tell of their experiences that weekend. They would use a microphone and speak in front of the group.

Sometime later, the same presentation was given to the youths at the Sacred Heart Church in Detroit.


Follow-Up

There were also follow-up meetings with these children at the correctional facility at a later date. The meetings were called "Ultreya," which means a place to come together to encourage and support. They were taught that the word also meant "onward."

They would assemble in a room, and talk about how things had gone since that weekend, and how their thinking and habits had changed.

The children were so drawn to this movement that they asked if they could write to the members. Some did, and they always received a letter back.

Other Faith-Based Experiences

During Mr. Nanni's involvement with this group, he witnessed one participant work as a healer on two occasions. Her deeply rooted faith and connection with God allowed her to place her hands upon a young girl with leukemia and later her sister with cancer, while praying, and they were both healed.

Although Mr. Nanni has strong religious beliefs, he is open to accepting this faith healing as well as my spirituality. I am a visionary, and although I proclaim to be spiritual rather than religious, I have encountered many visitations in the mind's eye from revered figures of religion. I, too, have a strong connection with God and the spiritual world.

He wanted me to mention that I have authored several books in the category of psychic phenomena and spiritual encounters under the name Ellen Marie Blend, modeled after my late grandmother.

One year while on vacation, Mr. Nanni and I visited a Catholic church called the El Santuario de Chimayó. It is located in the Sangre de

Cristo Mountains of Chimayo, New Mexico.

The sanctuary is a **National Historic Landmark** that has been a place of worship since before its construction in 1813.

It is famous for the story of its founding and as a contemporary pilgrimage site. It is said that the sanctuary receives almost 300,000 visitors per year.

There are many stories about this church and its healing powers. There is a room dedicated to its healing dirt, which visitors may dig up and take with them.

We brought small plastic containers with us. While there, we lit candles and filled our containers with the healing dirt to take back home.

The picture of El Santuario de Chimayó was a gift from a dear friend who also visited there. You can see some of the healing dirt that she spread on the frame.

El Santuario de Chimayó

## Teaching Non-Violence

Dear to his heart, Mr. Nanni brought the teachings of Students Against Violence Everywhere (S.A.V.E.) into the youth homes in Detroit. This was a program that taught that violence is no good for anyone, and to learn to change your ways.

To emphasize its importance, ex-offenders were brought in to tell their stories.

One gentleman, who was missing a leg, came in to speak to the children. When asked what happened to him, he said, "I ran away from what I did, and got shot. That's how I lost my leg."

Another ex-offender became a minister, and came to tell his story.

Although the *Barrington Bunny* and the *Ragman* are faith based stories, the principles of compassion, self worth and good conduct are among many other attributes that are present in both.

To stress the significance of these stories, students were to write, in their own words, what the stories meant to them.

# Who's Who
# Among American
# Teachers

One of Mr. Nanni's students who had difficulty in middle school became an honor student when he went to high school.

He was actually doing college work while in high school, and he went on to go the University of Michigan. He graduated with "cum laude" (Latin for "with great honor").

It was a total surprise when Mr. Nanni received a letter informing him that he had been nominated to be in Who's Who Among American Teachers by a student.

This student was so appreciative of Mr. Nanni's teaching methods and interest in his students' learning, that he entered his name in the book honoring the nation's most respected teachers.

Mr. Nanni was truly gratified and said, "While it's wonderful to be recognized by a former student, I'm so happy that I made a difference in someone's life." He was quite honored to join a select 5% of our nation's teachers.

Over the years, he saw the standards of passing children diminish, and it went against his principles as a teacher. He was forced to pass students who didn't even complete their homework assignments.

When it came to his retirement, John Gretts, the man who taught him how to teach wrestling, was one of the speakers.

He stated that Barney Nanni's retirement will be a huge loss to the wrestling programs at Center Line and Wolfe Schools. During his twenty years of coaching wrestling, he only had one losing season.

His teams also won the Van Dyke Wrestling Tournament three times and finished as runner-up twice. He was the type of coach that all parents wanted their kids to have-- fair and understanding.

He also read the letter from the student who went on to wrestle at Alma College.

When it was Mr. Nanni's turn to speak, he said, "I'm really not ready to retire, but I think it's time." He couldn't say how he really felt about the failings of the educational system.

He continued by saying that it would give him the

opportunity to pursue his S.A.V.E. program, Students Against Violence Everywhere.

He formed his own ministry, and continued to spread the words of love and compassion to all.